Boandik Country Bush Tucker

By Uncle Ken Jones

Illustrated by Bindi Lee Day

We respect and honour Aboriginal and Torres Strait Islander Elders past, present and future. We acknowledge the stories, traditions and living cultures of Aboriginal and Torres Strait Islander peoples on this land and commit to building a brighter future together.

Library For All Ltd.

Muntries are miniature apples that look like berries. They fruit in early autumn.

③

Karkaala, also called pig face, is a succulent with edible fruit that tastes like salty apples. The juice from the leaves is also good for healing burns.

5

Cumbungi, also called thirr, are reeds whose roots and underground stems can be cooked or made into flour.

Kela are crayfish, or southern rock lobsters, that can be caught and cooked to eat.

Wapuwat, also known as abalone, can be eaten raw or cooked and is considered a delicacy.

Snotty gobbles are also called dodder plants. The fruit can be eaten and their vines woven into nets and ropes, or used as trampolines.

13

Ngirr, or the sheoak tree, has edible leaves, and timber that is good for making boomerangs and other tools. This tree and its many uses provides a strong spiritual connection for Boandik people to their Country.

Green whelk turban snails are a main food source on Boandik Country. They provide a sacred spiritual connection to Country when eaten.

Kokba are yellow-eyed mullet fish. They're caught either by hunting with spears or using traditional fish traps, especially when catching them in bulk.

20

Fresh water spiny crayfish are a tasty treat that are ready to hunt when the tree hills and freshwater creeks begin running with water.

You can use these questions to talk about this book with your family, friends and teachers.

What did you learn from this book?

Describe this book in one word. Funny? Scary? Colourful? Interesting?

How did this book make you feel when you finished reading it?

What was your favourite part of this book?

About the contributors

Uncle Ken Jones is from Mount Gambier, South Australia, and Boandik (Bunganditj) Country. He likes being outdoors with his family and friends, fishing, going bush, and visiting the beach. He loved scary stories as a kid, especially cautionary tales about the bunyip.

Bindi is a Noonuccal artist from Quandamooka country in South-East Queensland. Bindi's artistic journey has been marked by a modern style infused with storytelling that not only reflects her saltwater cultural roots but also pays homage to freshwater communities, forged through years of collaboration with traditional Aboriginal artists in central Australia.

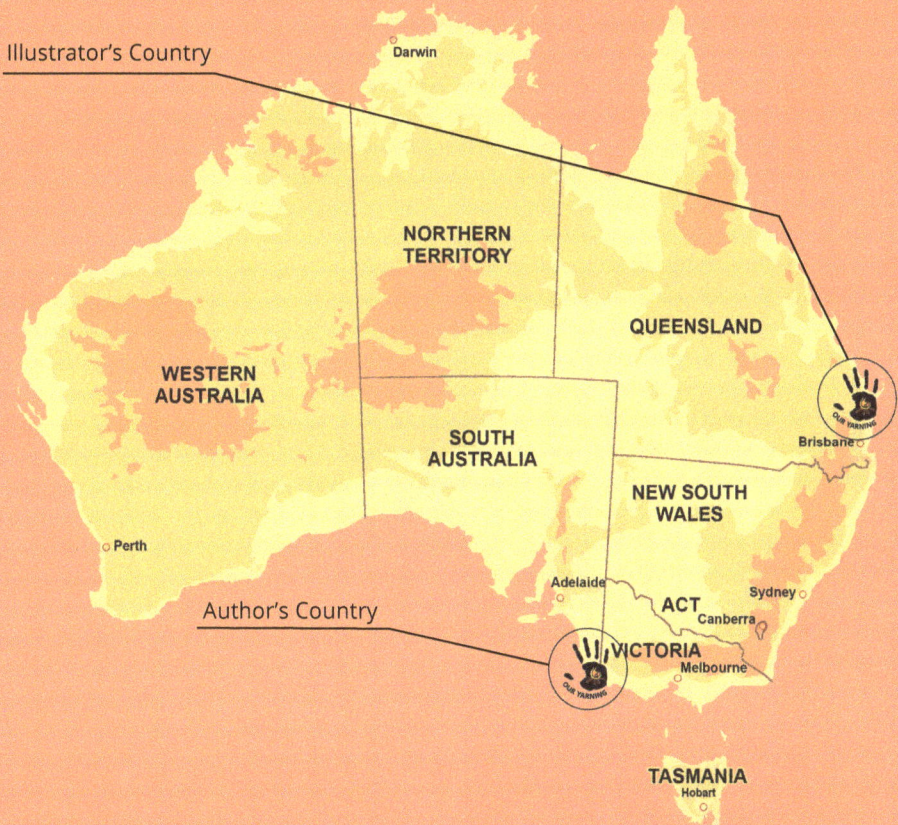

Illustrator's Country

Darwin

NORTHERN
TERRITORY

QUEENSLAND

WESTERN
AUSTRALIA

SOUTH
AUSTRALIA

Brisbane

NEW SOUTH
WALES

Perth

Adelaide

Sydney

ACT
Canberra

Author's Country

VICTORIA
Melbourne

TASMANIA
Hobart

Our Yarning

The Our Yarning collection aligns with the Australian Curriculum through the Cross-Curriculum Priorities — Aboriginal and Torres Strait Islander Histories and Cultures. The collection provides an authentic opportunity for learning and embedding Aboriginal and Torres Strait Islander perspectives because it is written by Aboriginal and Torres Strait Islander people.

We know that children learn better, and enjoy reading more, when they see themselves in the stories, characters and illustrations of the books they read.

To download the app, visit the Google Play Store or Apple Store and search 'Our Yarning'.

You're reading Level 2

Learner – Beginner readers
Start your reading journey with short words, big ideas and plenty of pictures.

Level 1 – Rising readers
Raise your reading level with more words, simple sentences and exciting images.

Level 2 – Eager readers
Enjoy your reading time with familiar words, but complex sentences.

Level 3 – Progressing readers
Develop your reading skills with creative stories and some challenging vocabulary.

Level 4 – Fluent readers
Step up your reading skills with playful narratives, new words and fun facts.

Middle Primary – Curious readers
Discover your world through science and stories.

Upper Primary – Adventurous readers
Explore your world through science and stories.

Boandik Country Bush Tucker

First published 2025

Published by Library For All Ltd
Email: info@libraryforall.org
URL: libraryforall.org

Our Yarning logo design by Jason Lee, Bidjipidji Art

Original illustrations by Bindi Lee Day

Boandik Country Bush Tucker
Jones, Uncle Ken
ISBN: 978-1-923554-47-4
SKU04913

www.ingramcontent.com/pod-product-compliance
Lightning Source LLC
Chambersburg PA
CBHW042342040426
42448CB00019B/3383